THE DARK HISTORY OF

ANCIENT
ROME

THE DARK HISTORY OF

ANCIENT
ROME

Sean Callery

 **Marshall Cavendish**
Benchmark
New York

Published by Marshall Cavendish Benchmark
An imprint of Marshall Cavendish Corporation

Website: www.marshallcavendish.us

This publication represents the opinions and views of the author based on Sean Callery's personal experience, knowledge, and research. The information in this book serves as a general guide only. The author and publisher have used their best efforts in preparing this book and disclaim liability rising directly and indirectly from the use and application of this book.

Other Marshall Cavendish Offices:
Marshall Cavendish International (Asia) Private Limited, 1 New Industrial Road, Singapore 536196 • Marshall Cavendish International (Thailand) Co Ltd. 253 Asoke, 12th Flr, Sukhumvit 21 Road, Klongtoey Nua, Wattana, Bangkok 10110, Thailand • Marshall Cavendish (Malaysia) Sdn Bhd, Times Subang, Lot 46, Subang Hi-Tech Industrial Park, Batu Tiga, 40000 Shah Alam, Selangor Darul Ehsan, Malaysia

Marshall Cavendish is a trademark of Times Publishing Limited

All websites were available and accurate when this book was sent to press.

Library of Congress Cataloging-in-Publication Data

Callery, Sean.
    The dark history of ancient Rome / by Sean Callery.
        p. cm.—(Dark histories)
    Summary: "A collection of dark deeds from the ancient and medieval world"—Provided by publisher.
    Includes bibliographical references and index.
    ISBN 978-1-60870-084-4
    1. Rome—History—Juvenile literature. I. Title.

    DG77.C305 2010
    937—dc22

                                2009033477

Editorial and design by
Amber Books Ltd
Bradley's Closeose
74–77 White Lion Street
London N1 9PF
United Kingdom
www.amberbooks.co.uk

Project Editor: Sarah Uttridge
Design: Andrew Easton
Picture Research: Terry Forshaw and Natascha Spargo

PICTURE CREDITS:

FRONT COVER
Colosseum: Dreamstime/Million Matthieu
Caesar Augustus: Photos.com
Mourning Augustus: Getty Images/Hulton Archive

BACK COVER
Death of Spartacus: Mary Evans Picture Library

AKG Images: 3 (Peter Connolly), 17, 22, 23, 32 (Electa), 34, 37, 42 (Peter Connolly), 44, 45, 48 (Erich Lessing), 49, 52, 55, 56; Bridgeman Art Library: 6 (Look & Learn), 8 (Private Collection), 10 (Look & Learn), 14 (Museo e Galerie Nazionali di Capodimonte), 18 (Musee des Beaux Arts Andre Malraux/Giraudon), 26 (Private Collection), 28 (Look & Learn), 31 (Museo Archeologico), 38 (Private Collection), 46 (Bonhams), 50 (Joanna Booth), 51 (Tretyakov Gallery); Corbis: 33 (Alinari Archives), 35 (Araldo de Luca), 36 (Stapleton Collection), 40 (Araldo de Luca), 54 (Michael Nicholson); De Agostini: 16; Dorling Kindersley: 43 (Ermine Street Guard); Dreamstime: Background image 2/3 (Valeria Cantone), 13 (David Harding), 30 (Ron Sumners); Mary Evans Picture Library: 20, 21, 24, 58; Getty Images: 15 (National Geographic Creative), 27 (Hulton Archive), 59 (Hulton Archive); Photo12.com: 57 (Oronoz); Photos.com: 11; TopFoto: 12 (Granger Collection), 41 (Alinari Archives); Werner Forman Archive: 25

Printed in China

135642

Contents

Chapter 1   Dark Beginnings   7

Chapter 2   Power Crazed   19

Chapter 3   Commodus   29

Chapter 4   The Soldier Emperor   39

Chapter 5   Dark Days for Christians   47

Chapter 6   Fight to the End   53

Glossary   60

Key Figures   62

Find Out More/About the Author   63

Index   64

Dark Beginnings

A ncient Rome was a highly successful civilization but it was built on injustice and violence. The Roman **Empire** lasted more than a thousand years beginning in 753 BCE, growing to span 2,500 miles (4,025 kilometers) from Britain to Africa. It is remembered for achievements including wonderful **architecture**, art, establishing organized **government** and the rule of law, and for building towns and road networks.

However, beneath this civilized surface was an unequal society. One-quarter of its people were **slaves** with no rights or freedom. A small group of families held onto power most of the time, and were more than willing to kill anyone, including their own relatives, if their position was threatened.

Roman cities were carefully planned and well organized. Those who wished to rule them arranged killings to get their enemies out of the way.

A Dark Legend

The ancient **myth** of the founding of the city of Rome starts with dark deeds. According to the legend, twin brothers, Romulus and Remus, were born in 771 BCE to the daughter of King Numitor. His brother Amulius wanted the throne for himself so he ordered a servant to drown his nephews so they could not inherit power. Instead, the servant floated the boys down the Tiber River in a cradle. The twins were found and raised by wolves and then by a shepherd.

In 753 BCE the boys decided to build a city on one of the seven hills near where they had been found. But they argued about where it should go. Romulus plowed a furrow and told his brother not to cross it because it marked the edge of his **territory**. When Remus leaped across the line, Romulus swung his sword and killed his twin. He then went on to build Rome, naming the city after himself.

Romulus and Remus, the founders of the city of Rome, were cared for by wolves. They were later looked after by a shepherd and his wife.

Rock of Death

A slave caught stealing would be killed, but the method of execution for this, and for other serious crimes such as murder and **treason**, was particularly gruesome. The condemned person was taken to the Tarpeian Rock, a steep cliff on top of the Capitoline Hill overlooking the Roman **Forum**, the hub of the city. Then they were thrown off it, plunging nearly 130 feet (40 meters) to certain death on the sharp rocks below. Bodies were then thrown into the Tiber River to rot, where fish then fed on them. This method was also used on people with mental or physical disabilities because it was believed the gods had cursed them. Criminals from noble families were luckier—they were strangled.

Tough Laws

By 550 BCE Rome was a **republic** where the people elected their rulers. At the center of its government was the Law of **Twelve Tables**, a set of rules by which people had to live. Some rules didn't seem too harsh. For example:

- If you failed to repay a debt, you could be put in fetters (leg irons) with a minimum weight of 15 pounds (7 kilograms).

- If you attacked a man and broke one of his bones, you had to pay him three hundred donkeys. If you hurt a slave just as badly, you only had to give half as many animals to his owner.

Some laws tried to match the punishment to the crime:
- If you burned down a house or grain store the punishment was the **scourge** (whipping) and then being burned to death.

Others showed who was boss in the family:
- Fathers had the right to kill their sons, and all deformed babies were to be put to death.

Some laws changed based on the time of day:

• If you caught a thief during the daytime, you had to shout for help. But if it was at night, you were allowed to kill him.

Sliced Eyelids and Spiked Barrels

Punishments were more hands-on during the long-running war between Rome and the African city-state of Carthage. Both sides committed grisly acts. When a Roman high officer called Marcus Atilius Regulus was taken prisoner he was treated very badly. Stories were told that his eyelids were cut off and he was laid out in the sun so that its rays burned

his eyes. It was also said that he was pushed into a barrel into which spikes were driven. As he tried to hold his body away from their sharp points, the container was rolled along the street. His body would have been punctured repeatedly as the barrel tumbled along.

When the Romans finally defeated Carthage after years of war in 146 BCE they took fearsome revenge. The city of Carthage was captured and burned, and then the charred ruins were smashed into the ground. Some historians believe

Roman officer Regulus was nailed inside a spiked barrel that was then pushed down the street. It was a gruesome and very painful method of execution.

that salt was plowed into the surrounding fields so that nothing could grow. It could be said that the men who were slaughtered in the attack were luckier than the 50,000 women and children who lived. All survivors of Carthage were sold into slavery.

Terrible Punishment

In 71 BCE an even more public act of revenge was used to show the people of Rome how ruthless its leaders could be. A man called Spartacus led an army of slaves in a revolt against Rome. After a series of battles, the Roman army defeated the rebels, butchering thousands at Brundisium in southern Italy.

They were the fortunate ones. Six thousand captured slaves were marched along 266 miles (428 km) of roads that led to Rome in the north. They were forced to carry crosses. Every so often during the march, those at the back of the line were nailed to the cross they were carrying and mounted on the side of the road to die

Spartacus, a trained slave gladiator, led a revolt against the Roman Empire.

a slow, agonizing death. The corpses were left on the crosses, picked at by the crows and allowed to rot. For years the road was lined with skeletons still hanging from the crosses, serving as a very powerful warning to other rebels.

New Emperor, Fresh Blood

When a new **emperor** came to power two things were certain and they both involved bloodletting. The new emperor would declare a public holiday and put on special **gladiator** games to celebrate the victory and thank his supporters. And his enemies would suffer.

When Sulla gained power in Rome, he ordered the killing of those who could threaten him. Anyone who helped or sheltered his victims was also punished by death.

One blood-soaked example was when Lucius Cornelius Sulla fought his way into Rome and gained power in 82 BCE. He then killed anyone he considered a threat, proclaiming them enemies of the state. It is thought that 9,000 were killed in a few months, including 1,500 members of the nobility.

Many nobles condemned by a new emperor chose to kill themselves by cutting their wrists or falling onto their own sword rather than be executed. It was in their interest to do this because if they committed suicide, their property was still owned by their family and could be passed on. If the state killed them, their lands went to the emperor because they were seen as **traitors**.

Hail Caesar

Julius Caesar is one of the most famous Roman rulers. This is partly because his reign marked the end of the Roman republic and the beginning of the age of emperors who took power for themselves.

He was a ruthless and cool operator. For example, in 75 BCE Sicilian pirates, who were well known for their brutality, captured Caesar. But the young general was more than a match for them. First, he told them he was too important for their ransom of twenty talents, and would arrange for them to be paid fifty. Then, while held on their ship for thirty-eight days,

Julius Caesar was a politician and soldier who began a civil war in 49 BCE and became the leader of the Roman world.

Caesar's murder was so frenzied that some of his assailants struck each other in the confusion. His body was stabbed twenty-three times.

he acted as if he was in charge of them, making speeches and demanding quiet when he wanted to sleep.

The ransom was paid and he was released. Caesar returned and captured the pirates, taking them to the local governor to be punished. When that didn't happen he decided to punish them himself. He snatched them out of jail and crucified them on the shoreline where passing ships would see their fate. It was no surprise that such a proud and ambitious man wanted power.

Caesar hated being told what to do and employed a gang of thugs to scare people who complained about him. Early on in his reign, he got annoyed with a critical **senator** (top politicians of the day) called Bibulus and the unfortunate man had a bucket of human waste emptied over his head.

Caesar started a bloody civil war, defeating his rivals to become Rome's **dictator**, the sole ruler. But there were many who did not want Rome to have what was in effect a king. On March 15, 44 BCE, a date known as the Ides of March, Caesar was murdered.

It was a messy death. The senators (including many who had been his friends) led him into a room, pretending they wanted to show him a document. Suddenly one of them pulled down Caesar's tunic while another lunged at his neck with a dagger. The rest of the group drew their knives and stabbed their leader while he fell twitching to the ground in a pool of blood. There were twenty-three stab wounds on his body.

Tiberius

The story of Tiberius shows the terrible results of a madman who became emperor and behaved just as he liked with no one willing to challenge him.

Tiberius was a great general who came to rule the Roman world from 14–37 CE. To maintain his political power he was forced to leave the wife he loved and to marry his stepsister Julia. He got rid of her as soon as he could. After he began his rule as emperor he put Julia under house arrest, meaning she could not leave her home. Tiberius ordered the guards not to allow her any food and she died a slow and painful death from starvation. He later also killed his mother and his two sisters because he thought they were a threat to his rule.

His most trusted aide was a soldier called Sejanus who led the emperor's bodyguards, known as the **Praetorian Guard**. Sejanus was cunning and secretly desired to become the next emperor instead of Tiberius's son, Drusus. He befriended Drusus' wife, Livilla, and

Tiberius was a harsh ruler, killing those who he considered his enemy.

told her that he was more likely to get and stay in power than her own husband. He was so persuasive, and she wanted so much to be part of the ruling group, that she agreed to help him poison her own husband, Drusus. It was a long, slow, and painful death that took several days.

For a while, the arrangement worked. Tiberius was happy to let Sejanus rule on his behalf because he trusted him. But after eight years it became clear to him that Sejanus was a rival and not a friend and had been involved in the killing of Drusus. In 31 CE Tiberius had Sejanus strangled and his body left in the middle of Rome. People knew what Sejanus had done and kicked his body to pieces, feeding the flesh to dogs and crows.

Villa of Violence

At various times in his rule Tiberius went to live in a huge villa on the island of Capri in the south of Italy. Here he had wild parties and devoted his life to idle pleasure. But an invitation to join him there could be a death sentence. If he decided someone was an enemy and not a friend, he had them tortured and thrown off a cliff into the sea. Just in case they survived the drop, a group of sailors waited in boats and broke up the bodies with boat hooks.

No Surprises

A fisherman once alarmed Tiberius by suddenly appearing in front of him, offering him the best fish in his catch. But Tiberius, terrified of being attacked, was frightened when he realized the man had clambered across rocks to get to him. He punished the poor man by rubbing the fish across his face, digging its sharp scales into his skin. When the fisherman thanked his lucky stars that he had not offered an enormous crab he had caught, Tiberius had his face torn by the crab's claws as well.

Left to Rot

Meanwhile, Tiberius ordered the deaths of all who he considered to be his enemies— and there were a lot of them. They were grabbed with a sharp iron hook and dragged away to be strangled. The bodies were left on the street or thrown into the Tiber River. Their relatives and friends did not dare to remove their decaying bodies in case they too were accused of conspiring against Tiberius.

Eventually Tiberius became dangerously sick. The next emperor in line, Caligula, sped things along by arranging for him to be killed by placing a pillow over his face to suffocate him. At last, as Tiberius had always feared, he was assassinated, but his death was a lot more peaceful than those of his many victims.

When Tiberius discovered Sejanus was plotting against him, he had him arrested and executed, along with many of his friends and family.

Chapter 2

Power Crazed

The first five Roman emperors had a lot in common. They were all from the same power-crazed family, the Julio-Claudians, and they all had many people killed to keep their grip on the throne. And most of them went insane.

The strangest was Caligula, which is not surprising when you consider the terrible things that happened around him as a child. His father, Germanicus, was poisoned on the orders of Tiberius. He lived with his mother until the crazy emperor decided she could no longer be trusted. She was banished along with Caligula's brothers, but Tiberius seemed to like Caligula and brought him and his sisters to live in Capri. They were no more than prisoners there, watching Tiberius torture his enemies and no doubt wondering if they were next.

The great fire of Rome burned for seven nights, destroying much of the city and damaging the reputation of the Emperor Nero.

Emporer Caligula

Caligula came to power in 37 CE when the old emperor died (probably suffocated by Macro, an aide of his who was also friends with Caligula). He ruled very well until he was struck down by a terrible illness. Many thought he was going to die. He recovered, but he had changed into a completely different person and behaved like a madman. Suddenly he enjoyed cruelty and killing. For example, a Roman nobleman called Artanius Secundus had said he would

Caligula was a harsh ruler who enjoyed torture and killing. He lived his life as if it was one long party.

Little Boots

Caligula's real name was Gaius Julius Caesar Augustus Germanicus. But he was given the nickname Caligula when he was very little. He loved to dress up as a soldier, with a proper helmet and tiny sandal-like boots such as those worn by the troops. This is how he got his name Caligula, which means, "little boots."

Walk on Water

An astrologer had once said that Caligula had no more chance of becoming emperor than of riding his horse over the Gulf of Baiae, a bay on the Italian coast that was 3 miles (5 km) long. In 39 CE Caligula decided to show the astrologer how wrong he was. He sent for cargo ships and arranged them in pairs across the bay before having them covered with earth to form a bridge. Then he spent two days riding back and forth across the bay. This stunt caused a grain shortage for a while afterward because there were no boats available to deliver it.

gladly fight as a gladiator if the gods spared the emperor. So Caligula sent him into the ring (he survived). Another, named Potitus had said he would give up his life to save Caligula. So he was put to death. Many others were killed or forced to take their own lives, including his closest advisor, Macro.

From then on Caligula lived his life as if it was one long party. He spent huge sums of money on ships decorated with jewels, massive new palaces, and held spectacular games. He liked money so much that sometimes he would have a pile of gold poured onto the street so that he could roll around in it. He had to raise new taxes to pay for all this wild spending but they didn't bring in enough. So, he made up stories that rich men had committed crimes and then made them pay enormous fines in order to avoid punishment.

Caligula grew so fond of Incitatus, his horse, that he dined with it.

Short Temper

Caligula was very cruel to anyone who annoyed him—and he was easily annoyed. Senators were forced to wait on him like a slave, or race alongside his **chariot**. Nobles who offended him were branded with irons before being sent to work in the mines. The usual method of execution was strangling or cutting off the head, but that wasn't nasty enough for Caligula. He liked to watch, sometimes over a meal, while victims were killed slowly with lots of tiny cuts so that their death was slow and painful.

Once at a party a slave was caught stealing some silver thread from a couch. Caligula

Caligula had an obsession with the moon. He would cry out at the full moon shining down, trying to call up the Roman moon goddess Diana.

had his hands cut off and strung round his neck. Then the thief was marched around the party behind a sign saying what he had done.

A Living God

Previous emperors had been named as gods after they died, so Caligula went a step further and decided he was a living god and must be worshipped. He had two temples to himself built in Rome. One had a life-sized golden statue of himself that was dressed in the same clothes that he wore each day. Caligula began to dress up as Roman gods, such as the superhero Hercules or the huntress Diana. This was particularly ridiculous because he was a terrible general and had had little success at war, even though he pretended he was a hero. In fact, after one disastrous battle he dressed some people up as captives and paraded them through the streets to make it look as if he had triumphed.

CLAVDIVS CAES.

Claudius is depicted here as a conquering hero. In reality he was not a successful soldier: he walked with a limp and he drooled when he spoke.

The insanity couldn't last. A guard called Cassius Chaerea, whom Caligula had mocked because of his high voice, led the plot that killed the bizarre emperor. It was similar to the **assassination** of Julius Caesar. Cassius and his comrades waited to ambush him in a narrow passageway near the games he was attending on January 17, 41 CE. They took turns stabbing Caligula with their daggers. It was a far quicker death than those he had enjoyed watching at mealtimes.

Another Killer

When Caligula and most of his family and friends were killed, his uncle, Claudius, seemed to have expected that he, too, would be murdered. A guard found him hiding behind a curtain in the imperial palace and told him he was the new emperor. Claudius didn't seem like a leader.

Saving Slaves

One of Claudius' decisions shows one of the many dark sides to the Roman system of slavery. Masters whose slaves were sick used to take them to the temple of Asclepius, the Greek god of healing. They were abandoned to die but if they survived the masters expected them to come back into service. Claudius ordered that if they lived, they could be free. This did not go down well with the ruling class who were already annoyed that Claudius had brought in lowly people to help run the government.

He spoke with a stammer and limped around on thin legs that were probably damaged by an illness such as polio.

But he turned out to be rather a good emperor whose biggest sin was overeating but, this being ancient Rome, he couldn't hold onto power without shedding some blood. There were many plots against him and he is said to have been responsible for the deaths of thirty-five senators and three hundred knights (powerful businessmen).

The Romans were famous for their feasts. They drank wine and dined on plates of peacock tongues and stuffed mice.

Poisoned By His Wife

However, being a good ruler didn't mean you were popular or would avoid assassination—even by your own family. In the end, either eating bad mushrooms or his doctor pushing a poisoned feather down his throat killed Claudius. It is likely that his own wife (who was also his niece), Agrippina, arranged this to ensure that her son Nero became emperor, rather than Claudius' own child Britannicus.

Bad Dad

Nero's father, Gnaeus Domitius Ahenobarbus, didn't set a very good example to his son. During his life he:

- Purposely drove his chariot over a child who was playing with a doll on the street of a village on the Appian Way.
- Took out the eye of a knight who spoke against him.
- Stole prize money from the winners of chariot races.
- Cheated merchants he dealt with.

Marry and Die!

Marrying Nero was pretty much a death sentence, because his wives did not survive long. First came Octavia, whom he divorced and then had killed when there was a public outcry at how badly he had treated her. He then married Poppaea but kicked her to death during an argument about his coming home late from the chariot races. She was pregnant at the time. He executed the husband of Statilia Messalina so that he could marry her. Sadly, all this time the woman he loved most was a freed slave called Claudia Acte, who was his mistress. However, an emperor could never marry an ex-slave. Nero bribed officials to say she was a noble, but everyone knew it was a lie.

First Prize

Nero was convinced he was a brilliant public speaker and musician, and nobody dared to say that his voice was actually thin and reedy. The Romans often held music festivals and competitions in making speeches. Nero always won because the judges were frightened of him. No one was allowed to leave during his performances, which could go on for hours. He played the lyre, a small harp. Sometimes he is pictured playing a violin, but this had not yet been invented.

Nero insisted on performing his music for hours at a time. Audiences were too frightened not to applaud him and were not allowed to leave before the end.

A Plot of Death

His mother had put Nero in power because she thought she could rule through him. But he was uncontrollable so she started plotting to get rid of him and have Britannicus made emperor. Nero heard of this and acted ruthlessly. He paid a woman called Locusta to make a poison that would be hard to detect so that he could secretly kill his rival. She did, but it was working too slowly. Nero got tired of waiting so he ordered her to make a faster-acting poison. This was slipped into fourteen-year-old Britannicus' drink.

The liquid was barely past the poor boy's lips before he froze and fell to the ground twitching. Nero said he was just having a fit and to let him die. But his mother Agrippina knew the truth and, true to form for a member of the Roman nobility, began plotting to have her second cousin, Rubellius Plautus, put on the throne.

Beds and Boats

Nero found out and decided to kill his mother and make it look like an accident, but his methods were ridiculous. First he thought of a special ceiling that would fall and crush her in bed, but that was too complicated. Then he had a boat adapted to break up at sea and sent her on a voyage. It sank, but she swam to safety. When the messenger came with this news, Nero had another idea. He claimed the man was an assassin sent by his mother and had her killed for trying to murder him. Once she was dead he was so relieved that he held a special celebratory procession through the streets of Rome.

The End of the Insanity

Nero loved spending money on big projects for himself. In 64 CE much of Rome burned down in a terrible fire. Many hundreds died and most of the buildings in the city center fell down. Nero put up taxes to pay for the damage and had a huge palace built over the ruins, complete with a lake, parks, and fountains. Some suggested that he had arranged the fire to clear space for this huge folly, known as Domus Aurea. There were rebellions in parts of the Roman Empire and Nero became so unpopular that the **Senate** declared him a public enemy and proclaimed a new emperor. He fled and killed himself on June 9, 68 CE, rather than be caught and beaten to death. At last the insanity was over.

Nero wanted to avoid the shame of being publicly flogged to death, so he decided to take his own life instead.

Chapter 3

Commodus

L ots of little children like to run around with a toy sword and pretend to fight. The Roman emperor Commodus did this as an adult, except his weapons were real and no one was allowed to hit back. Commodus never really grew up and was allowed to pretend to be a gladiator in the famous arena of the **Colosseum** in battles that only he was allowed to win.

The cruel side to his character was revealed early on. When he was twelve a servant prepared his bath with water that was too cold. In his fury the shivering Commodus ordered that the man be thrown into the blazing furnace to kill him for his mistake. A slave threw in a sheepskin instead and convinced his master that the meaty smell of it burning was the bath keeper's flesh cooking.

Chariot races were one of the most violent events in the Roman Games. Riders wrapped the reins round their bodies so if they fell they would be dragged along by the horses.

The Colosseum

The Romans loved to watch fights between gladiators and among wild animals at special oval **arenas** called **amphitheaters**. The most famous and largest one was the Colosseum in Rome. It could seat 50,000 spectators who watched fights and spectacles, such as chariot races. The emperor often paid for these events as a gift to the public. Commodus, however, was the first emperor to actually take part as a gladiator.

The Work Shirker

Commodus wasn't much of a thinker and did not relish having to do the work of an emperor, preferring to play sports and leave the job to his advisors. He spent much of his time enjoying himself at home, especially after he was frightened by an assassination attempt, which were common at this time. The first major one came in 182.

As would-be assassin, Quintianus, walked toward Commodus, he pulled out his sword. He showed his weapon too early and was stopped by the guards, but not before he had shouted, "This is a message from the Senate." That showed there were important people behind the plot. This being Rome, it might come as no surprise that these included Commodus' own sister, Lucilla, and probably his wife, Crispina, plus two of their cousins. Soon they were all dead.

Corrupt Cleander

Commodus had given many of his powers to his close friend Saoterus, but he was found dead. Next to get the job was Cleander—a freed slave who worked for

Commodus expected to be worshipped like a god and felt he was like the mythical hero Hercules.

the emperor and the man who had arranged the killing of Saoterus, without his master knowing. Cleander was corrupt and greedy, and happy to take bribes in return for favors. If you wanted a top job, you paid Cleander for the post. If a trial judge decided against you, you paid Cleander to change the result. Cleander became a very rich man, but he always made sure Commodus got a share of the money.

But when food ran short in 190, Cleander got the blame because of his poor organizational methods, and an angry mob of people threatened him while he was watching a horse race at the Circus Maximus. Cleander ran to his emperor for safety, but Commodus was so frightened at the sight of the furious crowd that he had Cleander beheaded right there. The crowd carried away the body and stuck Cleander's head on a pole to display around the city. Commodus went on to kill any nobles he suspected of plotting against him. He even executed two innocent men from the Quintili family, Conianus and Maximus, just in case they became a threat. They were not actually involved in plots against him, but, the emperor reasoned, they were wealthy and clever and so might be tempted to do him harm in the future.

Types of Gladiator

There were many kinds of gladiator. They used different equipment and had different ways of fighting, such as:

• **Dimanchaerius:** equipped with two swords and some light armor.
• **Retarius:** carried a net to catch his opponent like a fisherman. Had armor on his left arm and shoulder. Carried a trident (three-pronged spear) or a harpoon to continue the fisherman theme.
• **Samnite:** wore a crested helmet and carried a sword and shield. This slowed him down, but he was well protected.
• **Secutor:** had a light shield and a short sword. He would chase his opponent and try to catch them off balance.
• **Velitus:** armed with just a spear and no armor, so had to be quick.

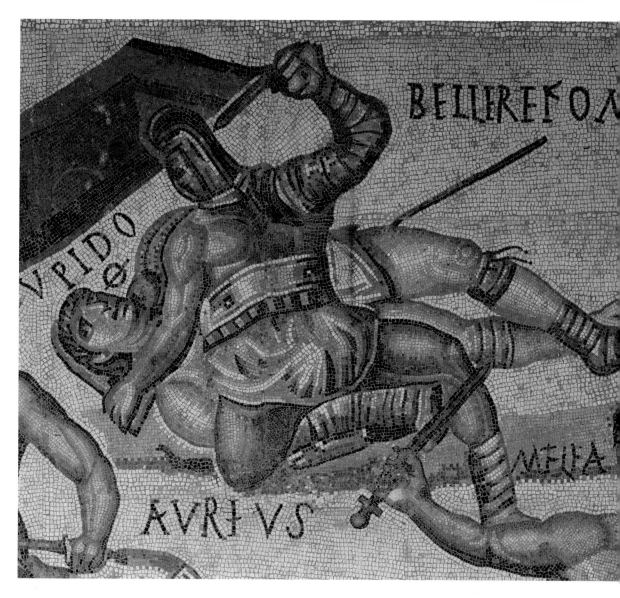

The Emperor Gladiator

The most popular form of entertainment in Rome was gladiator fighting. Commodus was fascinated by it. He trained with gladiators, and fought in the arena in front of the public.

Successful Roman gladiators were as popular as film stars today but their job was dangerous and they were only a step away from death in the arena.

Gladiators were often convicted criminals, prisoners of war, or slaves, although some were free men such as ex-soldiers who chose to fight for money. They were used as thugs during elections, when candidates would hire them to threaten **citizens** with violence if they did not back the right person.

Sometimes gladiators fought alone and others fought as part of a team. Gladiators did not always battle to the death. When one was wounded and knew he could not win the battle he would raise his left hand with the first finger pointed to ask for mercy. The crowd would shout out whether he should live, depending on how popular he was and how bravely he had fought. The emperor would make the choice, possibly by showing his thumb. The emperor or, in his absence, a judge would make the choice. He did this by pointing his thumb up or down. It is thought thumbs up was the signal for death (possibly instructing the gladiator to thrust his sword up into the guts) and the thumbs down meant spare him.

Dead End

If the decision were death, the loser would grasp the thigh of his opponent who would stab him in the neck to finish him off. Then attendants dressed in costumes as Charon (the

Land and water

Different forms of fighting were popular at various times. From the years 55–200 there were some women gladiators who only fought each other or animals. At other times, for variety, gladiators might wear a helmet with no eyeholes and work by sound alone. Or they might fight on horseback or from chariots, or from ships in a flooded arena. A typical day's events would start with an animal hunt, then executions of convicted criminals, and finally some man-to-man fighting.

FEMINÆ.

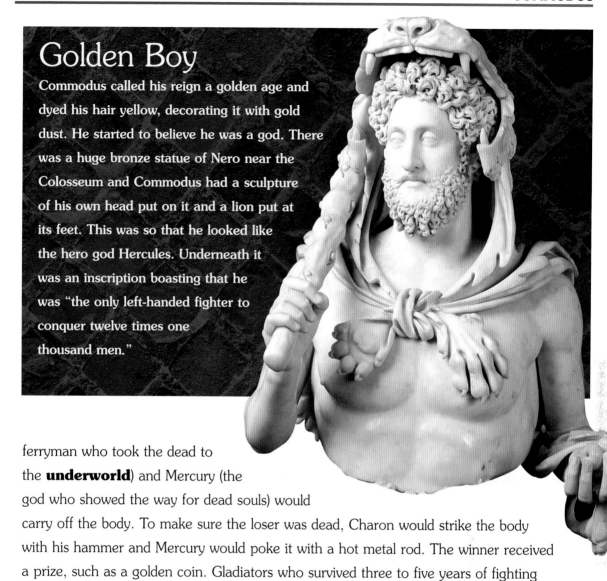

Golden Boy

Commodus called his reign a golden age and dyed his hair yellow, decorating it with gold dust. He started to believe he was a god. There was a huge bronze statue of Nero near the Colosseum and Commodus had a sculpture of his own head put on it and a lion put at its feet. This was so that he looked like the hero god Hercules. Underneath it was an inscription boasting that he was "the only left-handed fighter to conquer twelve times one thousand men."

ferryman who took the dead to the **underworld**) and Mercury (the god who showed the way for dead souls) would carry off the body. To make sure the loser was dead, Charon would strike the body with his hammer and Mercury would poke it with a hot metal rod. The winner received a prize, such as a golden coin. Gladiators who survived three to five years of fighting were freed.

Commodus adored the whole gory business and appeared as a gladiator 735 times. His opponents were only given blunt weapons and of course they did not dare fight hard enough to defeat the emperor, so they were defenseless. In public fights, he would generally spare his defeated competitor, but in training fights he was not as restrained and was likely to kill the unfortunate opponent.

Animal Hunts

Animal hunts were very popular, especially if they involved exotic animals from faraway lands. Beasts that were fought included elephants, crocodiles, bulls, big cats such as lions, leopards and tigers, and even ostriches. Sometimes they were pitted against each other.

Elephant fights were particularly popular, but there are also records of other contests such as bulls being put in the arena with a bear or rhinoceros.

Commodus was a very keen animal hunter. Unlike the venators (animal fighters), he would usually fight from a platform built around the arena so that the animals could not attack him, so it was no more than target practice with a spear or a bow and arrow. But he was skilled. In one day he killed one hundred lions with one hundred spears, so he didn't miss once. He was such an accurate archer that he could shoot the head off a sprinting ostrich.

Commodus fires his arrow to kill the escaped leopard. He loved to be portrayed as a hero.

Dangerous Tablet

No one was safe from Commodus. His mistress, Marcia, found out for herself, with a deadly consequence. When Commodus told her he intended to march the streets of Rome with his friends the gladiators she was horrified. She begged him not to lower his status as emperor by doing it. Commodus was so annoyed by this that he added her name to a list of people to be executed the next day. Marcia found the list and saw her own name on it. Now it was him or her that must die.

Clean Break

That night, as usual, she took Commodus a glass of wine to have in his bath. She watched him sip the drink with its extra ingredient of deadly poison that she had poured in, and then fall asleep. She must have thought the job was done. But suddenly he awoke and threw up. Maybe his body was getting rid of the poison. Marcia acted fast. She sent for Narcissus, the professional wrestler who was the emperor's fitness coach, and promised him riches for the terrible task she wanted him to do. Soon his strong hands were around his master's neck, strangling the breath out of him as he gasped and choked.

No one mourned the death of Commodus. The Senate voted to destroy statues and pictures of the gladiator emperor, and pretend that he had never existed.

Commodus renamed Rome the Colony of Commodus. When he died his statues were destroyed and Rome got its name back.

Chapter 4

The Soldier Emperor

It is not unusual for brothers to fight. But the brothers Caracalla and Geta were joint Roman emperors and—when they fought—there was big trouble. Their father Septimius Severus was a tough general who had seized power in 197 and brought stability where there had been chaos. He was a strong ruler. It was clear that power would stay within the family, so the brothers' future looked secure.

But, of course, there can only be one emperor. Caracalla was the oldest, born in 188, a year before his brother Publius Septimius Geta. So it was natural that he was named as the successor of Severus. But the brothers had always argued and Geta didn't want to be second best.

Geta sulks in the background as he watches his brother Caracella with distrust. It was inevitable that one would eventually kill the other.

Unhappy Marriage

Their mother, Julia, was very clever. In fact, she helped to rule from Rome while her husband did what he liked best, which was fighting for the empire. But women were not supposed to rule so she had to work alongside his best friend Plautianus. There was a problem: Julia didn't trust him as much as her husband did. Seeing the danger of Plautianus trying to take over power, she arranged for her eldest son Caracella to marry his fifteen-year-old daughter Fulvia Plautilla so that they were part of the same family. But Caracalla was only seventeen and not ready for marriage. He was often in a bad mood and had a terrible temper. The two were very unhappy together and argued all the time.

Plautianus was afraid that the marriage would end, risking his position. So he decided he would have to kill Severus and his family and seize power for himself. Julia and Caracalla learned of the plot and told Severus. There could be only one result: Severus had his best friend executed on January 22, 205.

Stay Together

Severus saw how his sons disliked each other and decided the safest thing to do was keep the whole family together under his control. The squabbling brothers lived with him in Campania, in southern Italy, for two years.

Caracalla was a mild-tempered youth but when he grew up he became impatient and quick to anger.

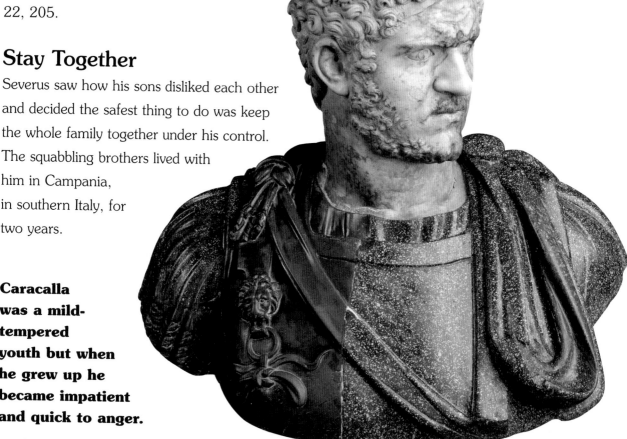

Bickering Brothers

After their father, Severus, died, Caracalla and Geta were free to argue as much as they liked. They had different friends. They competed with each other on who could behave the worst, holding wild parties and spending lots of money. When they both took part in a chariot race, Caracalla fell and broke his leg. No doubt Geta hoped the injury was more serious as he rattled past his injured brother.

Then in 208 they all joined him on a trip to Britain, a faraway place on the edge of the Roman Empire. It was a disaster. The brothers still argued constantly. There was a strange incident when Caracalla and his father were riding ahead of their soldiers to talk peace with a group of Scottish rebels. Caracalla suddenly raised his sword and seemed about to use it on his own father. But the emperor's bodyguards shouted a warning and he put it back in its sheath. That

Geta fought his brother all his life and in the end was killed by him—the Roman Empire wasn't big enough for them both.

evening Severus called his son, handed him a sword, and challenged him to kill him if he really wanted to. Caracalla just shook his head.

They were still in Britain in 211 when Severus became very ill. He called his sons to him and gave them some advice: "Be harmonious, enrich the soldiers, and scorn all other men." The emperor died soon after. Caracalla was to remember that guidance.

Tough and Obedient

Like his father, Caracalla loved being among soldiers. He marched with them and ate the same food. Roman soldiers were tough and obedient—they had to be. They were trained to march 20 miles (32 km) in five hours, carrying heavy equipment, because in battle they had to move together. The punishment for not fighting was decimation: soldiers drew lots to select one out of every ten men. The other nine then had to club their comrade to death.

The two brothers returned to Rome and were proclaimed joint emperors. Neither would eat at the same table for fear that one brother would try to poison the other. When they went to the games they cheered for opposing teams. Whenever they met each was protected by personal bodyguards. The imperial palace was split into two, with separate entrances. They fought so much that they even considered dividing the empire in two, East and West, and ruling separately, but their mother Julia put a stop to that. She seemed to favor Geta as some others did, perhaps partly because he looked very much like his father. Caracalla was jealous of this, so he came up with a plan to end the problem.

An End to the Feud

On December 26, 211, Caracella told his mother he wanted to stop the feud and asked her to help. She was delighted and sent for her younger son to come without his guards to her apartment so that they could all talk. It was a death sentence. Caracalla had ordered his soldiers to kill Geta as soon as he arrived. Seeing their raised swords he rushed to his mother, but he died in her arms as the guards hacked at his body.

Everyone knew it was a planned murder even though Caracalla claimed Geta had been plotting to kill him. Would the army support this killer emperor? If they didn't, he couldn't rule.

Big Bribes

Caracalla knew how to ensure their support by following his father's advice to "enrich the soldiers." He made a huge gift of money to the Praetorian Guard, the part of the army that looked after the emperor. Each man got a bonus of 2,500 denarii and their food ration was increased. He later arranged a wage increase from 500 to 675 denarii to the other Roman soldiers. It was a huge bribe and it worked: he had the support of the army.

To finance these massive payments, Caracalla reduced the amount of silver in Roman coins to save money, and granted Roman citizenship for the first time to all the free men in the empire. Being granted citizenship, however, meant that they now had to pay taxes, so he received more income. Caracalla asked a highly respected aide called Papinianus to give a speech to the Senate saying that he had been forced to kill Geta. The man refused, and was soon dead, accused of treason. Knowing that the army would back him, Caracalla got rid of his other enemies. His wife Fulvia and her family were killed. For two weeks, his soldiers ran riot in Rome. It is thought they butchered as many as 20,000 people. The Senate did nothing because they knew it would mean death for them, too.

Roman soldiers were equipped with swords such as the gladius and the shorter dagger (pugio), which was also a common weapon for assassination as it could be hidden under clothes.

In 213 Caracalla fought tribes from Germany and offered their captured women a choice of slavery or death. Most chose to die.

The people of the Egyptian city of Alexandria did not believe Caracalla's claim to have acted in self-defense in killing his brother. Nor did anyone else. In Alexandria they performed a play mocking him. He took revenge in 215 in much the same way that he had defeated his brother. He arranged an official visit to the city, inviting its important people to a banquet. It was their last supper, for as the bowls were being cleared away Caracalla's soldiers rushed in and butchered every guest. Meanwhile the rest of his army landed and moved through the city house by house, slaughtering another 20,000 of its inhabitants.

The Enemy of Mankind

Caracalla fought alongside the Roman army for several years after he killed Geta. He was totally ruthless in battle, slaughtering civilians even after they had admitted defeat. Such was his cruelty that the distinguished historian Edward Gibbon said he was "the enemy of all mankind."

Foretelling the future was an important part of life in Rome, where fortune-tellers, known as soothsayers, had a lot of influence. One predicted that Caracalla's second in command, Macrinus, might one day become emperor. It was clear that Caracalla would see him as a threat and kill him. Macrinus seemed to have realized this and acted first.

Macrinius' guards were with the emperor on April 8, 217, as he went on a trip to the temple of Luna the Roman moon goddess. As Caracalla was climbing onto his horse a guard called Julius Martialis came to his side. It must have looked as if he was helping his master up onto the animal, but instead he plunged his sword into the emperor's stomach. Macrinus claimed he was so furious he immediately killed Martialis. It was a smart move. That meant no one could find out why he had done it, because dead men don't talk. Caracalla, the emperor who loved being among soldiers, had been killed by one of his own army at the young age of twenty-nine.

Caracalla was cut down by one of his own guards, Julius Martialis, who had pretended to help him onto his horse before sliding his sword into the emperor.

Chapter 5

Dark Days for Christians

Christians suffered terribly for hundreds of years in the Roman world. The Romans had numerous gods, many of them taken from the ancient Greeks. They believed that the gods chose their rulers and, in fact, most emperors were worshipped as gods after they died. So the Christian belief in one god was seen as highly dangerous because it challenged the right of Roman emperors to rule. This meant the Romans considered Christians to be traitors. They were treated as common criminals and, to the Roman mind, were inferior beings deserving of no mercy.

Christians had fewer legal rights and those who refused to take part in animal sacrifices were punished with prison or execution. Although this had happened for centuries, toward the end of Diocletian's reign (which ran from 284–305) this persecution reached new heights when about three thousand Christians were killed because of their faith.

In ancient Rome refusing to make a sacrifice to the emperor or Roman gods was seen as treason. As a result, Christians were killed in huge numbers.

Splashed with Blood

The Romans were very superstitious. They believed in omens and that occurrences such as lightning bolts were messages from the gods. When planning a major event, they would sacrifice an animal such as a sheep. Its blood would be collected and splashed over statues of the gods. Priests would examine the liver to look for signs of success or problems. Another method of telling the future was watching the behavior of birds. On one occasion, before a naval battle, the chickens on board a Roman boat refused to eat. After the battle was lost it was believed that the chickens had predicted this failure.

Word From the Gods

Diocletian ruled alongside other officials and they could not agree what action to take against the Christians. So in 302 they consulted an **oracle** (someone who was believed to be able to receive messages from

Under Diocletian the persecution of Christians was bloodier than ever and those meeting for worship risked death.

the gods). The reply was that the god Apollo could not speak because of "the just on earth." This was taken to mean that the Christians were preventing a Roman god from speaking. This could not be tolerated. Diocletian decided to punish them.

He was soon enforcing his decision. The followers of a Christian-style religion founded by the prophet Mani were punished according to their status. Those of low rank were beheaded. If they had higher standing they were sent to work in the marble quarries on Marmara Island, Turkey, cutting the rock that would be used in **pagan** temples.

The alternative—being sent to the copper and lead mines—was worse. It meant a lifetime of slave labor working alongside the worst convicted criminals. The mines were dark, hot, and dangerous. It was hard to breathe, and the air that did reach the lungs was heavy with metal poisons that caused paralysis or killed you. Working in these mines was a living death.

On February 23, 303, Diocletian ordered that a newly built Christian church at Nicomedia in Turkey be burned to the ground and all its books of scriptures set on fire. The next day he ordered the destruction of Christian books and buildings across the empire. From that point on, Christians could no longer meet to worship, or complain to the courts. This made it much easier to punish them, often with the scourge (see sidebar, p. 50). Even local judges were allowed to sentence Christians to death.

The most common method of execution was to tie them to a wooden stake and burn them alive. They were also sometimes killed as part of the entertainment at a gladiator show. The Romans toyed with their Christian victims the way a cat plays with a mouse before killing it.

Because they were seen as outsiders, Christians were often blamed for things that went wrong. Once, a fire destroyed part of the imperial palace and the blame was put on the Christians even though there was no evidence at all for this. A group of them

The prophet Mani founded a religion which became one of the most widely held faiths in the world, but was challenged by the Roman state.

were accused of starting the fire and were quickly killed before anyone could ask too many questions about why, but one called Peter suffered a terrible death. He was stripped and whipped. Then salt and vinegar were poured onto his open wounds. Finally, he was set over an open fire and burned to death.

History Repeats

The event was a terrible echo of one from the summer of 64 during the reign of Nero. A fire burned in Rome for a week and almost three-quarters of the city was destroyed. Many blamed Nero, so he ordered the arrest of some Christians as scapegoats to shift the accusations off of himself. They were tortured until they would say anything to end their suffering and blamed other Christians. That gave Nero an excuse to round up all the members of the Christian sect and kill them. He used this as an opportunity for entertaining the people of Rome. Some were fed to wild animals. Others were crucified, while some were burned alive at the stake like human torches. Such was their suffering that the Romans, who usually enjoyed watching a gory death, started to feel sorry for them.

A few hundred years later, in November 303, Diocletian was attending an official sacrifice when a deacon (a Christian official) called Romanus shouted out a protest that he felt the ceremony was wrong. He was grabbed and tied to a stake. However, Diocletian was so furious at the interruption he decided to increase the punishment. Romanus' tongue was cut out so that he could no longer voice his protest. He was then tortured in prison for some time before being finally strangled.

Nailed to a Cross

Another common way of killing Christians (and other criminals) was

The Scourge

The scourge was a leather whip with pieces of metal tied to it. When it struck the body it ripped off the skin, leaving a bleeding mess of raw flesh and exposed muscles. There was no limit to the number of lashes dealt, and victims were often whipped until they were near death.

crucifixion. Victims were whipped with a scourge and then tied or nailed to a cross where they were left to die, which could take many hours or even days. Victims might perish from the shock and pain, loss of blood from their wounds, or infection.

Some people believe another cause of death on the cross was the inability to breathe as the sagging body crushed the lungs. Sometimes when the victim had been on the cross for a while their legs would be broken by force. This would mean they died more quickly from shock and loss of blood. One variation on the method was to turn the cross upside down. Crucifixion was a horrible death because it was slow, painful, and happened in public.

Fed to the Lions

Another method of execution—being fed to lions or other wild beasts such as savage dogs—was just as public, but much faster.

Crucifixion was seen as the worst kind of death because it was public. It also involved terrible suffering.

The first victim of this is thought to be the Bishop of Antioch, Saint Ignatius, in 107. He refused to worship the Roman gods and was brought to the Colosseum in Rome. There he was pushed into the arena, closely followed by two lions.

Another Christian who died in the Colosseum perished because he annoyed the crowd. Telemachus was a monk from Egypt. He went to the famous arena in 404 and was shocked by the slaughter that he saw. He stepped out onto the sand and shouted at the spectators. This made them so angry that they threw rocks at him and stoned him to death. Other accounts suggest it was the gladiators who finished him off. Either way, he is credited with ending the gladiatorial contests because they were banned soon after this incident.

By this time, Rome had become a Christian empire. Earlier, in 312, Emperor Constantine converted to Christianity and it became the main faith in the empire soon afterward.

Chapter 6

Fight to the End

The Roman Empire could not survive forever. Its army was too weak and stretched out too thinly along the long borders of the Empire. In the fifth century it was divided into two kingdoms, West and East. If anything, this increased the amount of plotting and intrigue to get power. With small sections of the empire up for grabs, there were more prizes to aim for and more people in the way. In the Roman Empire, you could trust no one, not even members of your family. In fact, they were often the greatest threat.

When the East Germanic tribe the Vandals reached Rome in 455 they spent fourteen days plundering and wrecking the city. The Roman Empire was almost dead.

Power Struggles

The power struggles around the time of the rule of Valentinian III illustrate how dark deeds were a way of life in Roman politics. It was a twisting tale of lies, betrayal, and murder.

Part of the Family

Valentinian was the son, grandson, great-grandson, cousin, and nephew of Roman emperors, so the role of Augustus (the title used for Roman rulers) was in his blood. That didn't mean he was suited to a role as leader, though. In fact, he seems to have been manipulated at every stage of his life and rule. It started early. He was betrothed to be married at the age of four to form an alliance. His bride-to-be was two years old at the time. He was only six when he was installed as Roman Western Emperor in October 425.

Obviously he wasn't in charge. His mother took on much of the role, working with officials and generals from the army. Her name was Galla Placidia. She was the daughter of an emperor, Theodosius I. She knew the ways of power and plots. Placidia grew up in the household of a powerful general, Stilicho and it was agreed when she was a tiny child that she would marry his son Eucherius, linking their families together.

More Plots and Deaths

Placidia and Eucherius never wed. Theodosius I died in 395 and as usual there

VALENTINIEN III
EMPEREUR D'OCCIDENT.
450-55.
IVOIRE DE LA CATHED.LE
DE
MONZA.

The reign of Valentinian III saw the loss of vast areas of the Roman Empire.

were plots and counter plots over the succession. The empire was divided into East and West, and Stilicho became commander in chief of the Western army. He was later accused of conspiring to put his son on the throne of the Eastern Roman Empire, which may well have been true. He was beheaded on August 22, 408, and Eucherius was rounded up and killed soon after.

The incident led to the besieging of Rome by a Germanic tribe known as the Goths. Placidia was among those who were trapped in the city. She was already an expert in the art of politics. When her own cousin Serena was accused of plotting with the rebels she agreed with the decision of the ruling body, the Senate, to execute the traitor. Then she was

When the Goths sacked Rome in 410 it was the first time in nearly eight hundred years that the city had fallen to an enemy.

a victim of dark deeds herself, captured by the Goths and forced to marry their leader Ataulf in January 414. But her husband was murdered in his bath a year later in revenge for the death of a German chieftain, Sarus.

Back in Power

Placidia returned to Italy and lived with the emperor, her half brother Honorius. Placidia was powerful but when she disagreed with Honorius over a political appointment, brother and sister had an argument and she fled to Constantinople with her son and daughter, probably afraid of assassination.

When Honorius died (of natural causes, which was pretty lucky if you were emperor) in 423, the infighting started again. An official named Joannes seized power, but a Roman

Honorius was a weak emperor who is shown here being bothered not with the affairs of his fading empire but with feeding his pet pigeons.

Secret Letter

Aetius and Boniface were powerful and ambitious generals and in Rome that meant each needed to get rid of the other. Aetius came up with a sly plan. He told Placidia that Boniface was building a dangerous power base in Africa and was a threat to Rome. He told her she could prove this herself by telling Boniface to come to see her. If he were loyal he would come, otherwise he was plotting something.

Meanwhile Aetius secretly wrote to Boniface warning him that Placidia suspected him of treason, and advised him to ignore the invitation to Rome that she was sure to send.

Sure enough, the invitation arrived and Boniface refused it. His friends in Italy were amazed and persuaded Placidia to let them meet Boniface and find out what the problem was. When they saw the secret letter from Aetius, the plan was revealed. The two generals finally came to blows when their armies fought each other at the battle of Rimini in 432. Boniface's forces won, but he was injured by a spear and died a few months later. Aetius was sent into **exile** but returned to Italy a year later.

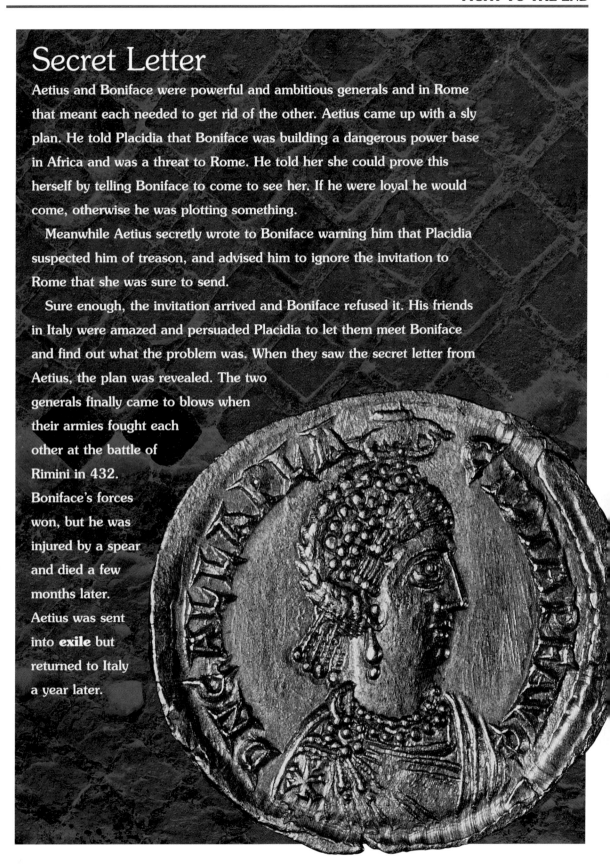

FLAVIUS AËTIUS.

ATTILÆ HUNNORUM REGIS TERROR.

Ex antiquo marmore, teste Julio Strozza.

Aetius had the skills needed of a Roman emperor: he was a good soldier and politician. But like others he was killed by a rival.

general known as Count Boniface refused to accept him. From his base in Libya, he had a powerful weapon—the grain that fed Italy. Boniface stopped the export from Africa of this important food, threatening to starve the center of the Roman Empire.

A rival general, Aetius, gathered an army of 60,000 men to support Joannes but reached Ravenna (which had replaced Rome as the center of power) three days after the self-proclaimed emperor had been executed on Placidia's orders. It was a horrible death. They cut off his hand, paraded him on a donkey to be insulted by the people, and then chopped his head off.

Placidia paid off Aetius' army and gave him a job as military commander, installing her son Valentinian III as Western Emperor at the age of six. Then she ruled in his place.

By the time Placidia died in 450, Aetius was hugely powerful, and he won great acclaim in finally defeating the attacks of another rebel group led by Attila the Hun in 451. In 453 he betrothed his son Gaudentius to marry Valentinian's daughter. It looked as if Aetius' position was secure.

New Enemies

But he had new enemies. A senator called Petronius Maximus and the emperor's chamberlain, Heraclius, wanted him out of the way and told Valentinian that Aetius wanted to put his own son on the throne. Valentinian knew that meant death for him and decided to strike first. He called Aetius to a meeting. As the general started to read from his notes, the emperor rose up and plunged his dagger into his enemy.

More Arguments

Now it was the turn of Maximus and Heraclius to argue as the chamberlain won their power struggle, leaving his rival out in the cold. Maximus would not tolerate that and added two soldiers who had been loyal to Aetius to the imperial guard. On March 16, 455, as Valentinian practiced his archery skills, the two assassins struck, killing him and the horrified Heraclius. It didn't do Maximus much good. He proclaimed himself emperor but within two months an East Germanic tribe called the Vandals attacked Italy. In the chaos, abandoned by his guards, Maximus tried to escape. An angry mob recognized him and took revenge. They stoned him to death and threw his body into the Tiber River.

After one thousand years of dark deeds, the exhausted Roman Empire finally collapsed in 476.

Aetius defeated Attila, king of the Huns, in 451. But he didn't block off the mountain routes to Italy so Attila later invaded and destroyed several cities.

Glossary

Amphitheater
An oval open-air arena for public shows.

Architecture
The design and construction of buildings. Romans were famous for the building of roads, aqueducts, and arches.

Arena
A building where gladiatorial games were held.

Assassination
The organized killing of a public figure.

Chariot
A cart with two wheels pulled by horses used in ancient Rome.

Citizen
A free person who was allowed to vote.

Colosseum
A huge amphitheater in Rome where animal fights, games, and gladiator bouts took place.

Crucifixion
A method of execution where a person is nailed to a large wooden cross and left to hang until they die.

Dictator
A ruler with total power.

Emperor
The ruler of an empire.

Empire
Different lands ruled over by a single person or government.

Exile
To be away from one's state or country, either by being threatened by death or imprisonment upon return or refused permission to return. Often used as a form of punishment.

Forum
Open space in the middle of a town for markets and meeting people (such as a market square).

Gladiator
A trained slave or captive in ancient Rome who was trained to fight to the death in a public arena.

Government
The system by which a country or state is ruled.

Myth
A story that may or may not be true, often very old.

Oracle

Someone believed to receive messages from the gods.

Pagan

Someone who believes in more than one god.

Praetorian Guard

The part of the army that protected the emperor.

Republic

A state in which power belongs to the people, rather than a king or other ruler.

Scourge

A whip used for punishment.

Senate

The Roman government, made up of senators.

Senator

A person elected to be part of the government.

Slave

Someone who is forced to work for no pay and has no rights. They are often held against their will.

Territory

A defined area of land that is considered the possession of a person, state, or country.

Traitor

Someone who commits treason.

Treason

The crime of betraying a leader or country.

Twelve Tables

An early set of laws that gave rights to the people of Rome.

Underworld

A gloomy place where Romans believed their soul went after they died.

Key Figures in *The Dark History of Ancient Rome*

Aetius	Emperor from 433 to 454
Attila	Emperor of the Huns from 434 to 453
Boniface	Roman General, known as one of the last Romans
Julius Caesar	One of the most famous rulers. He reigned from 49 to 44 BCE.
Caligula	Emperor from 37 to 41 BCE
Caracalla and Geta	Joint emperors from 211 to 217
Cassius Chaerea	A centurion in the army of Germanicus. He assassinated Caligula in 41 BCE.
Claudius	Emperor from 37 to 41 BCE
Commodus	Emperor from 180 to 192
Diocletian	Emperor from 284 to 286
Heraclius	Emperor from 610 to 641
Honorius	Emperor from 395 to 423
Joannes	Emperor from 423 to 425
Petronius Maximus	Emperor from March 17, 455 to May 31, 455
Nero	Emperor from 54 to 68 BCE
Galla Placidia	Daughter of Emperor Theodosius I and half-sister to Honorius (392–450)
Marcus Atilius Regulus	Roman High Officer
Romulus and Remus	Founders of Rome in 753 BCE
Sejanus	Bodyguard and close friend of Emperor Tiberius
Spartacus	Led an army of slaves in a revolt against Rome in 71 BCE
Lucius Cornelius Sulla	Roman general and politician (138–78 BCE)
Tiberius	Emperor from 14 to 37 BCE
Valentinian III	Emperor from 425 to 455

Find Out More

BOOKS

Deary, Terry. *The Rotten Romans* (Horrible Histories). New York: Scholastic, 2007.

Reece, Katherine. *The Romans: Builders of an Empire* (Ancient Civilizations). Vero Beach, FL: Rourke Publishing, 2006.

Schomp, Virginia. *The Ancient Romans* (Myths of the World). New York: Marshall Cavendish, 2009.

WEBSITES

Odyssey Online: Rome
www.carlos.emory.edu/ODYSSEY/ROME/homepg.html

The Roman Empire in the First Century
www.pbs.org/empires/romans

About the Author

Sean Callery is a children's writer and teacher. He writes on a wide range of subjects including history, science, and the environment. He is also the author of *The Gem Guide to Dictactors*, the history section of the *Kingfisher Explore Encyclopedia,* and he contributed to *The Encyclopedia of Dinosaurs and other Prehistoric Animals*.

Index

Page numbers in *italics* refer to illustrations

Aetius, General, 57, 58, 59
Africa, 57, 58
Agrippina, 25, 26, 27
Alexandria, Egypt, 44
Amulius, 8
animal hunts, 34, 35–36
animal sacrifices, 48
animals, Christians killed by, 50, 51
Apollo, 48
Artanius Secundus, 20–21
Ataulf, King of the Goths, 56
Attila the Hun, 58, 59

Baiae, Gulf of, 21
Boniface, Count, 57, 58
bribery, 31, 43
Britain, 41
Britannicus, 26–27
Brundisium, 11
burning alive, 49, 50

Caesar, Julius, 13–15
Caligula, Emperor, 17, 19–23
Campania, 40
Capri, 16, 19
Caracalla, Emperor, *38*, 39–45
Carthage, 10–11
Cassius Chaerea, 23
chariot races, *28*, 30
Charon, ferryman of the
    dead, 34–35
Christianity, Rome adopts, 51
Christians, persecution of, *46*, 47,
    48–51
Circus Maximus, 32
cities, 6
citizenship, 43
Claudia Acte, 25
Claudius, Emperor, 23–25
Cleander, 31–32
coinage, 43, *57*
Colosseum, *30*, 51
Commodus, Emperor, 30, 31–32,
    36–37
    fighting gladiators, 29, 33, 35
Conianus Quintili, 32
Constantine, Emperor, 51
Crispina, 31
crucifixion, 11–12, 14, *46*, 50–51

decimation, 42
Diana, hunt and moon goddess, 22, 23
dimanchaerius gladiators, 32
Diocletian, Emperor, 48–49, 50
Drusus, 15–16

elephants, 35, 36

Eucherius, 54, 55
executions, 9, 10, 11–12, 14, 22,
    34, 58
feasting, 24
Fulvia Plautilla, 40, 43

Gaudentius, 58
Germanic tribes, *44*, *52*, 55, 59
Germanicus, 19
Geta, Emperor Publius Septimius, *38*,
    39–43, 44
Gibbon, Edward, 44
gladiators, *11*, 21, 33–35
    Christians killed by, 49, 51
    Commodus fighting with, 29, 33,
        35
    types of, 32
gladius sword, *43*
Gnaeus Domitius Ahenobarbus, 25
Goths, 55–56

Heraclius, 58, 59
Hercules, 31, 35
Honorius, Emperor, 56
Huns, 58, 59

Ignatius, Saint, Bishop of Antioch, 51
Incitatus, *21*

Joannes, Emperor, 56, 58
Julia, mother of Caracalla, 40, 42
Julius Martialis, 44–45

Law of Twelve Tables, 9–10
Libya, 58
Livilla, wife of Drusus, 15–16
Lucilla, sister of Commodus, 31

Macrinus, 44–45
Macro, 21
Mani, prophet, 48, *49*
Marcia, mistress of Commodus, 37
Maximus Quintili, 32
Maximus, Emperor Petronius, 58–59
Mercury, 35

Narcissus, 37
Nero, Emperor, 19, 25–27, 49–50
Numitor, King, 8

Octavia, wife of Nero, 25
oracles, 48

Papinianus, 43
pirates, 13–14
Placidia, Galla, 54, 55–56, 57, 58
Plautianus, 40
poisoning, 25, 26–27, 37
Poppaea, wife of Nero, 25
Potitus, 21

Praetorian Guard, 15, 43
pugio dagger, *43*
punishments, 9–12, 22–23, 48
Quintianus, 31

Ravenna, 58
Regulus, Marcus Atilius, 10
Remus, 8
retarius gladiators, 32
Rimini, battle of, 57
Romanus, 50
Rome
    adopts Christianity, 51
    decline of, 53
    East and West empires, 53
    fall of, 59
    founding, 8
    great fire of, *18*, 27, 49–50
    sacking of, *52*, 55–56
Romulus, 8
Rubellius Plautus, 27

Samnite gladiators, 32
Saoterus, 31
Sarus, 56
scourging, 49, *50*, 51
secutor gladiators, 32
Sejanus, 15–16, 17
Serena, 55
Severus, Emperor Septimius, 39, 40,
    41
slaves, 7
    executions, 9, 11–12
    freeing, 24
    revolts, 11–12
soldiers, *42*, 43
soothsayers, 44
Spartacus, 11
Statilia Messalina, 25
Stilicho, General, 54, 55
stoning to death, 51, 59
strangulation, 9, 16, 22, 50
suicides, 13
Sulla, Emperor Lucius Cornelius,
    12–13
superstition, 48
swords, *43*

taxes, 43
Telemachus, 51
Theodosius I, Emperor, 54
Tiber River, 59
Tiberius, Emperor, 15–17, 19
torture, 49, 50

Valentinian III, Emperor, 54, 58
Vandals, *52*, 59
velitus gladiators, 32

women gladiators, *34*